Create and Share | Thinking Digitally

Building a Digital Footprint

By Adrienne Matteson

Published in the United States of America by:
CHERRY LAKE PRESS
2395 South Huron Parkway, Suite 200, Ann Arbor, Michigan
www.cherrylakepublishing.com

Series Adviser: Kristin Fontichiaro
Reading Adviser: Marla Conn, MS, Ed., Literacy specialist, Read-Ability, Inc.
Book Designer: Felicia Macheske
Character Illustrator: Rachael McLean

Photo Credits: © Africa Studio/Shutterstock.com, 7; © Andrii Oleksiienko/Shutterstock.com, 11; © wavebreakmedia/Shutterstock.com, 13; © Zaitsava Olga/Shutterstock, 17

Graphics Throughout: © the simple surface/Shutterstock.com; © Diana Rich/Shutterstock.com; © lemony/Shutterstock.com; © CojoMoxon/Shutterstock.com; © IreneArt/Shutterstock.com; © Artefficient/Shutterstock.com; © Marie Nimrichterova/Shutterstock.com; © Svetolk/Shutterstock.com; © EV-DA/Shutterstock.com; © briddy/Shutterstock.com; © Mix3r/Shutterstock.com

Copyright © 2020 by Cherry Lake Publishing
All rights reserved. No part of this book may be reproduced or utilized in any form or by any means without written permission from the publisher.

Library of Congress Cataloging-in-Publication Data

Names: Matteson, Adrienne, author. | McLean, Rachael, illustrator.
Title: Building a digital footprint / by Adrienne Matteson ; illustrated by Rachael McLean.
Description: Ann Arbor, Michigan : Cherry Lake Publishing, 2020. | Series: Create and share : thinking digitally | Includes index. | Audience: Grades 2-3.
Identifiers: LCCN 2019033410 (print) | LCCN 2019033411 (ebook) | ISBN 9781534159099 (hardcover) | ISBN 9781534161399 (paperback) | ISBN 9781534160248 (pdf) | ISBN 9781534162549 (ebook)
Subjects: LCSH: Social media—Management—Juvenile literature. | Digital communications—Juvenile literature. | Online identities—Juvenile literature. | Internet—Safety measures—Juvenile literature.
Classification: LCC HM851 .M3834 2020 (print) | LCC HM851 (ebook) | DDC 302.23/1—dc23
LC record available at https://lccn.loc.gov/2019033410
LC ebook record available at https://lccn.loc.gov/2019033411

Cherry Lake Publishing would like to acknowledge the work of the Partnership for 21st Century Learning, a Network of Battelle for Kids. Please visit www.battelleforkids.org/networks/p21 for more information.

Printed in the United States of America
Corporate Graphics

CHERRY LAKE PRESS

Table of Contents

CHAPTER ONE
Leaving Tracks 4

CHAPTER TWO
The Parts of Your Digital Footprint 8

CHAPTER THREE
Keep It Positive: Share with Care 12

CHAPTER FOUR
Keep It Private 16

GLOSSARY 22
FOR MORE INFORMATION 23
INDEX 24
ABOUT THE AUTHOR 24

CHAPTER ONE

Leaving Tracks

Imagine you are playing outside in the snow. Turn around and look at the path you took. Your boots leave a trail of footprints that tell the story of your day outside. These footprints show where you started, where you ran to, and where you stayed a while. There are too many footprints to count.

You leave a similar trail when you spend time on the internet. You use the internet on a computer, tablet, or phone. The websites you visit and the things you say and do leave an invisible path. This path is your **digital footprint**.

Your digital footprint is important. It is the part of you that the world can see online. Footprints you leave in the snow will disappear. But the digital footprint you leave online will always be there. This is why you should be **intentional** about how you present yourself online.

You leave invisible footprints every time you go online.

Some websites have a way to remember you. When you visit these sites, they mark your web browser with something called a cookie. It's not the yummy kind. This cookie is really a tiny program that helps websites learn more about who is visiting them. Cookies are invisible, so you might have dozens of them without even knowing it!

Some websites leave cookies on your computer!

ACTIVITY

Checking Your Browser History

Did you know that your **internet browser** remembers the websites you visit? The most popular browsers are Chrome, Safari, Firefox, and Internet Explorer. Your browser history is the list of websites you have visited recently.

Open up your favorite web browser and look at the menu across the top. Find and click on the word "History." Take a look at the list of websites that appears. Are there any surprises? Do you remember visiting those sites? Try visiting two or three of your favorite websites. Then check the browser history again. What changed?

Your digital footprint tells the world about you.

CHAPTER TWO

The Parts of Your Digital Footprint

The internet plays a big role in our lives. It is a great place to play, create, and connect with other people. You might create a *Minecraft* server where you play and build with your friends. Maybe your parents helped you create an Instagram account where you post funny pictures of your dog. You might even have a YouTube channel where you post videos of yourself singing and playing the guitar. All of those things are a part of your digital footprint.

Be respectful and responsible when you are gaming.

An MMOG, or massively multiplayer online game, is a special kind of online game. There are three ways you know you are playing an MMOG:

1. You need to log in to play.

2. There are lots of other people playing and you can talk to them.

3. You are all playing and exploring in the same world.

Popular MMOGs are *Fortnite*, *Roblox*, and *World of Warcraft*. The way you play and talk to other players inside an MMOG is also a part of your digital footprint.

Did you post a new picture of your dog on Instagram? Do you have a new video on YouTube? If so, you added something new to your digital footprint. Even chatting with friends in an online game adds to your digital footprint. So does liking another photo on Instagram. (Just remember to always ask a parent's or trusted adult's permission before posting anything online.)

Part of your digital footprint is created by the people around you. Did your friends or family post pictures and videos of you on their social media accounts? Their posts become a part of your digital footprint too.

Everything you post is part of your digital footprint.

ACTIVITY

Social Media

Popular **social media** sites and **platforms** are Instagram, Facebook, Snapchat, YouTube, and Twitter. You have to be 13 or older to join most social media sites without asking your parents. So you might not use social media a lot yet. Interview people you know who use social media. Ask them which platforms they like to use and why. Then **reflect** on their answers. Which ones would you like to try? Are you more interested in talking to people you know? Or do you prefer sharing pictures and videos you make with the world? What tools do you think will help you be the best version of yourself online?

What do you like to share?

11

CHAPTER THREE

Keep It Positive: Share with Care

You want to make sure your digital footprint reflects the best parts of you. A good way to do this is follow one simple rule every time you post something online: share with care.

Share with care means thinking before you post anything. Ask yourself first:

- Will this hurt anyone?
- Will I be proud of this tomorrow?

What kind of posts make you proud?

Always think before you share something online.

Will this hurt anyone?

Everyone gets angry and upset. And it's easy to say something hurtful or disrespectful online. You might get mean comments on your YouTube videos or Instagram pictures. When these things happen, you may want to say something mean back to them. But before you post, stop and ask yourself: "Will this hurt someone?" It is always better to keep your anger off the internet and out of your digital footprint.

Will I be proud of this tomorrow?

Let's say you have a very funny and embarrassing video of yourself and a friend. You know will get a lot of likes and views if you put it online. But should you? Remember to stop and ask: "Will I be proud of this tomorrow?" It's a lot of fun to post a video that people watch and share. But it may not be a video you want in your digital footprint forever. The video will also be a part of your friend's digital footprint. You should decide together whether to post the video or keep it just for yourselves.

ACTIVITY

Sharing Isn't Always Caring

Every time your friends and family post videos and pictures of you, they are adding to your digital footprint. How do you feel about that? Get out a piece of paper and make a T-chart. Title one side "OK to Post" and the other side "NOT OK to Post." Maybe you are okay with your parents posting pictures and videos of your dance performances. But you're not okay with them posting videos from practice. Maybe you don't mind if your friends share pictures of you. But you don't want them to **tag** you. After you make your lists, talk with your friends and family members about your choices. Ask them what they are okay and not okay with too.

Ask before you post!

CHAPTER FOUR

Keep It Private

It's important to keep information like passwords, your full name, and your location **private** when you go online. Privacy keeps you safe and protects your **identity**!

Always be careful about what you share with someone online. Information about who you are and where you are should stay private. To stay safe, follow these rules:

- Never share your full name, school name, address, or phone number.
- Never share where you are right now. Post photos and videos from school events and vacations after you get home.
- Before you create an account or **login** online, talk to a parent or trusted adult. Ask them to look at the website or **app** and give you their approval.

Never post your real name or location.

Follow the same rules when you include your friends and family in your posts. Following these rules will allow you to have fun online without putting yourself in danger.

Protect your digital footprint by keeping your passwords private. You don't want anyone else to log in to your accounts and post something in your name. Someone could use your passwords to get personal information from one of your accounts. Share your passwords only with your parents or guardians. Keep them secret from everyone else.

Your digital footprint will keep growing as you get older. Do everything you can to be safe and respectful online, just like in real life. Then you can make sure the online world sees how fantastic you are! Your digital footprint becomes more and more important as you grow older. It can potentially be seen by other people, like future colleges or bosses!

Your digital footprint lasts forever. Make it positive!

ACTIVITY

Create Safe Usernames and Passwords

USERNAMES

Websites and apps will ask you to create a login. You need the login to be safe and easy to remember.

It's okay to use the same username for more than one account. Do not use your real name or any real information about you (like your school name or city). On a piece of paper, **brainstorm** four or five usernames with words and numbers that describe you:

- soccerguy11
- supersciencegirl2
- QBwonderful25
- jellollama08
- realsillyworld7

Strong passwords keep your information safe!

SHHH!

ACTIVITY
Continued

PASSWORDS

You should have a different password for each account. The best passwords are easy for you to remember but hard for other people to guess. A good password:

- Has more than eight letters and numbers
- Is a mix of letters, numbers, and special **characters** (like $ and #)
- Does not include anything about you that someone can guess—like your birthday, name, pet's name, or address

Try making a sentence and then using only the first letter from each word. For example, "I love to make pizza and play guitar all day" becomes "iltmpapgad." Then replace a few letters with numbers and capital letters: "iL2mp&pGad."

Your turn! On a piece of paper, brainstorm four or five safe passwords.

GLOSSARY

app (APP) a computer program, usually on a smartphone or tablet

brainstorm (BRAYN-storm) to come up with ideas or solutions to problems

characters (KAR-ik-turz) numbers, letters, or special symbols

digital footprint (DIJ-ih-tuhl FUT-print) the record of one person's activities on the internet over time

identity (eye-DEN-tih-tee) the information that makes up who you are on the internet

intentional (in-TEN-shuh-nuhl) done on purpose; deliberate

internet browser (IN-tur-net BROU-zur) a program used to access the internet such as Safari, Chrome, Firefox, or Internet Explorer

login (LAWG-in) a username and password used to sign in to a website

platforms (PLAT-formz) social media tools such as websites or apps

private (PRYE-vit) belonging to only one person or group of people and not shared with anyone else

reflect (rih-FLEKT) to think carefully about something

social media (SOH-shuhl MEE-dee-uh) a website or app designed for talking and sharing with other people

tag (TAG) adding another user's name to a social media post

For More INFORMATION

BOOK

Cook, Julia. *The Technology Tail: A Digital Footprint Story*. Boys Town, Nebraska: Boys Town Press, 2017.

WEBSITES

Common Sense Education—Ready to Play Digital Passport?
https://www.commonsense.org/education/digital-passport
Learn more about how to think through tough situations online by playing these interactive games.

YouTube—Your Digital Footprint {Elementary}
htttps://youtu.be/7sw7Q5MMX6E
Discover more about your digital footprint by watching this informative video.

INDEX

anger, 14

browser history, 6, 7

Chrome, 7
cookies, 6

digital footprint
   adding to, 10, 15
   parts of, 8–11
   and privacy, 16–19
   sharing with care, 12–15
   what it is, 4–5

Facebook, 11
Firefox, 7
footprint, digital
   See digital footprint
Fortnite, 9

identity, 16
information, personal, 16, 18
Instagram, 8, 10, 11
internet, 4, 8
Internet Explorer, 7

location, 16
login, 16, 20

Minecraft, 8
MMOG (massively multiplayer online game), 9

passwords, 15, 18, 20, 21
platforms, 11
privacy, 16–19

respect, 8, 19
Roblox, 9

Safari, 7
sharing with care, 12–15
Snapchat, 11
social media, 10, 11

tagging, 15
tracks, 4–7
Twitter, 11

usernames, 20

videos, 14, 15

websites, 4, 6, 7
World of Warcraft, 9

YouTube, 8, 10, 11

About the AUTHOR

Adrienne Matteson is a middle school librarian in Atlanta, Georgia. When she is not teaching her students to be good digital citizens, she is knitting, singing, serving the community, and doing her best to make a positive footprint of her own.